Vulgar Victorians

VULGAR VICTORIANS

Copyright © Summersdale Publishers Ltd, 2015

Images © Shutterstock or out of copyright

Summersdale Publishers Ltd
46 West Street
Chichester
West Sussex
PO19 1RP
UK

www.summersdale.com

Printed and bound in the Czech Republic

ISBN: 978-1-84953-791-9

3 4633 00324 1609

Vulgar Victorians

The Bad Behaviour of a Saucy Society

Belinda Hayward

summersdale

Introduction

Welcome to the world of *Vulgar Victorians*. A place where graceful ladies think the most disreputable thoughts. Where respectable-looking gents turn the air blue with unexpected ejaculations. Where the smutty meets the bizarre and goes to town dressed to the nines in a frock coat of funny filth. The pictures in the pages that follow finally reveal the real obsessions, perversions and peculiarities of a truly saucy society. And even when they weren't thinking about sex, their observations on food, music, sport and fashion were just as weird. So turn the page and begin your journey through the madness, the rudeness and the oh-my-goodness!

Eleonora hadn't had it in weeks, but Hugh insisted that he had 'one of his heads' yet again.

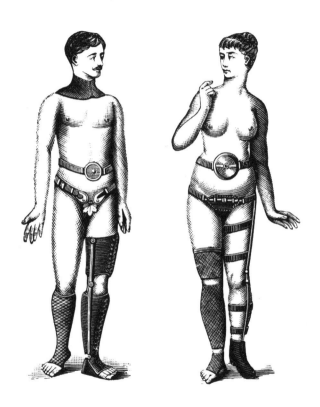

Hugo didn't know what type of party Fanny was taking him to, but she assured him he would have a good time.

Spencer's portable post-coital shower invention made him look like a bit of a douche.

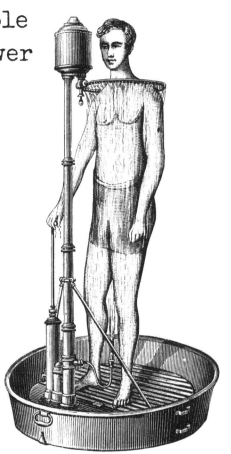

Sod those fishing regulations, thought Ted. I'm not throwing this one back!

Clementine wasn't sure what it was about Father's new cigarettes that made her so hungry but Mrs Widdershin's white soup was particularly moreish today.

'I don't care what you say; I still much prefer acid house to this newfangled dubstep nonsense.'

Fuck, thought Susan. One more waltz in this corset and I'm likely to vomit out my kidneys.

Albert knew from past experience that no one wanted a ride on an unkempt moustache.

Frederick refused to divulge how he lost his eye, other than saying it involved a goose, a flintlock pistol and a shit-ton of gin.

Mr Bunby was pleased to find that Bessie had a good, firm grip.

Goodness, how the 10th Regiment's rigorous burpee routine roused patriotic feelings within Wilhelmina's breast.

This time, the captain really had given Jones the horn.

Rupert would fight
any man who dissed his
skinny jeans.

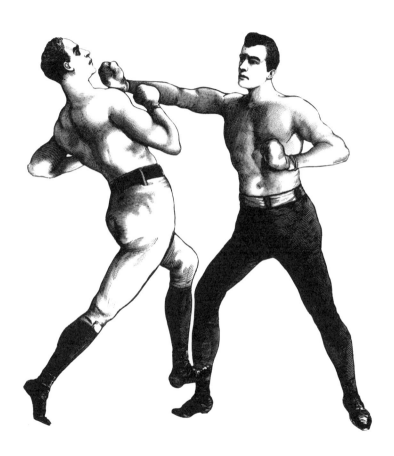

Miss Honeysham's buttered crumpets never failed to bring all the boys to the yard.

If Ada had to take one more 'quick' snap for tourists in Hyde Park, she was going to kick someone in the tits.

'My wife says I'm emotionally constipated,' laughed Alf. 'I haven't given a shit for days.'

'How could you possibly have run out of the dinosaur-shaped nuggets?!'

Emma wondered how much longer it would take her parents to realise that she meant 'dearest bosom friend' very literally.

Mrs Crumple's fingers brushed the narrow, waxy shaft of the candle and she suddenly found herself thinking of her dear departed Winston.

'I haven't seen my Mr Pee-Pee in twenty years – could you check it's still there, old boy?'

After spending the night with Mr Longfellow, Prudence wisely opted to ride side-saddle all the way home.

Fletcher knew without being asked that it was time, once again, to bring Lord Nombury a very large bucket.

Eliza side-eyed the crowd and said, 'I handle my men like I handle this cake.' What *had* Osbert got himself into this time?

'If you use plenty of baking soda, even the most dried-on jizz stains come out in the end,' boasted Granny Heather.

Name: Pippin

Occupation: Daddy owns some railroads.

Likes: Caviar, brandy, oysters on the balcony at sunset.

Dislikes: Non-shiny hats, having to pluck my ear hair, people who ask me what my occupation is.

Molly looked on fearfully: she knew that if Mr Fenton didn't praise Betsy's lemon posset, it was likely he'd be getting a painful taste of her copper pan.

Loretta found it hard to focus on her correspondence whenever the gardener's boy was working on the tender buds outside her window.

Having already ascertained the size of Herbert's bank balance, Hetty had decided that yes, she would let him ravish her tonight.

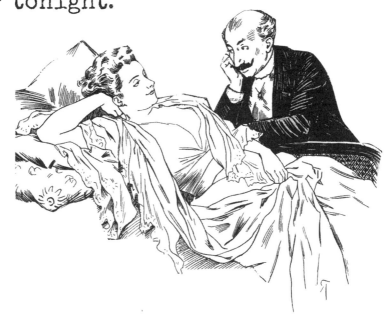

There was a certain frisson of danger to strip polo that Sadie relished.

'Nice jugs.'

'I know your boat's not very big but I'm sure we could all come at once if you give us a chance.'

Miss Fortescue
was famed around
town for the way
she handled a
stiff rod.

Roland couldn't bear to watch as the vicar stole away yet another one of his dates.

'No, I *am* looking at the letter, honest. But if you could just open your collar a little, you'd be so much more comfortable.'

'Unhand me,
you ruffians.
Oh stop, do.'

'There you are Mr Ripper, Sir.
All dressed up for your nightly
wanderings through the
London fog.'

William had deliberately chosen the back row of the theatre for its darkness, but he didn't know if he'd be able to penetrate Jessica's seemingly endless layers of clothing without a flashlight.

Kate spotted her rival's shoes: the very same she was sporting. *This means war, she thought. Her dance card is marked. For life.*

'TGI Friday!'

Bess had a patent. A patent for an elephant's toothpick. Now all she needed was investors.

Thanks to their new outfits, Algernon and Edmund felt sure of success in their plan to infiltrate the ladies' bridge circle.

Old Man Johnson was rather taken aback when the stranger sitting next to him in the park offered to get him 'higher than a motherfucking dirigible'.

‘Does this face look like it gives a shit?’

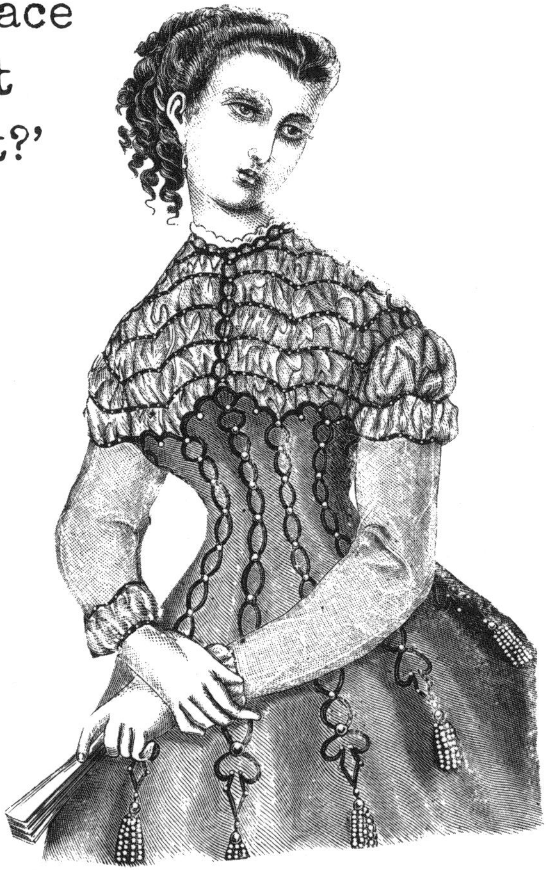

Budgets were tight again this year, but Matilda needed a new coat and the old picnic blanket still had plenty of wear in it.

'No really, this is just how long it takes,' Timothy mumbled as the busty triplets wondered why he was spending so long fiddling with his equipment.

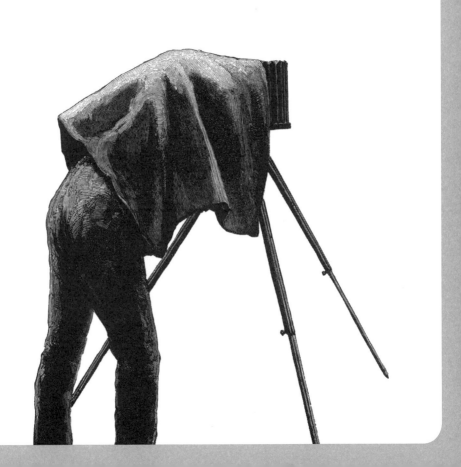

It was hard to know whether the flush of Stanley's cheeks was due to the excellent claret or the teasing pressure of the butt plug Quentin had inserted earlier that evening.

Coming home alone after another draining night's speed dating, Miss Finch allowed herself to accept Jane's ministrations once again.

Henry was hoping to get a good shot of Josephine's tunnel, too.

'How much wine is in this sauce?' asked George, conveniently forgetting his six-hour-long session at the gin house earlier that day.

Once again, the Ponsonbys found themselves scanning the small ads for a new housemaid. Preferably one who would be open to activities both upstairs *and* downstairs.

Belinda couldn't wait to display her muff to all the crowds at the ice-skating gala.

Grandfather said he was wasting his Cambridge education, but then Grandfather didn't appreciate the genius of his invention: the Real Ale Bong.

'I'll be frank,' explained Josiah, 'I don't know one end of a paintbrush from my arse, but the ladies soak their bloomers for an artist.'

Humphrey was a man
of few vices, but he did
like to stay up late
listening to sick beats
on the wireless.

Thirty years, six poison pen campaigns, two murders and a broken marriage later and here Wenceworth was. He had finally made it: second triangulist in the Whitby Amateur Wind Orchestra.

Nancy's corset did chafe somewhat, but the sensation of tightness was most agreeable.

Mortimer had heard that bondage could be fun. But after paying a princely sum to the nice lady, he wondered why the room had gone so quiet.

The town gossips all gathered to see the unveiling of Wandsworth Theatre's new show. Jemima thought it would be *As You Like It* but Dorothy still held out hope for the Chippendales.

*Wait till you see what I've got
planned for you,* bitch, thought
Beatrice, as she eyed the new
governess with a
pitying disdain.

While out
in Bengal,
Cyril got a
lot of pussy.

Miss Jacobs had possibly got carried away in her preparations for the Temperance Society's Halloween ball.

Barnaby and Alexander were elated: their new jazz mag was hot off the press and the centrefold babes were, quite literally, smoking.

'If you think this is OTT, wait till you see the topiary of my lady garden.'

Demelza began to seriously regret that fourth sherry when Bertie started twirling her on the dance floor.

'Aloysius,' Ronald sniggered under his beard, 'did you steal that belt from your mother's curtains?'

The lavish trips to the opera would continue, but Miss Carruthers had every intention of keeping Lord Darnley firmly in the friend zone.

Clarissa knew her one-piece bathing suit was extremely daring, but she had seen too many members of the Ladies' Swimming Club perish due to the sodden weight of their modesty petticoats.

The regulars at the Richmond BDSM Club knew they didn't have to ask whether new member Harriet was a 'top' or a 'bottom'.

Kenneth attempted to stifle his elation on seeing that the superglue on Arthur's chair was working like a charm.

Mr Greebling questioned whether streaks of warm white sauce should be floating in his beef consommé.

The Freddie Mercury tribute act was under pressure to win the weight-lifting competition and be the champion. The show must go on, and he didn't want to stop at all.

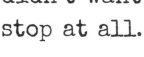

'If you look under my crinoline, you'll find my lower locks are equally impressive.'

'Just one shot,' they said. 'How bad could it be?' Then one turned into eleventy-one and Terence was once again absolutely pewtered.

'Can we not do this on the way to the Finchleys? I just want to enjoy a nice ride and a good meal with friends, but you still want to talk about that damn chambermaid. It was three years ago, Agatha!'

Lawrence always preferred to wear his drum as low as possible. Oh, how those vibrations thrilled through his loins as he marched across the parade ground.

Bella was very good at controlling her temper, but something about the way she was holding her parasol told Edwin *not* to raise the subject of the housekeeping bills with her today.

Name: Sylvie

Age: Don't you know it's rude to ask a lady?

Talents:
Piano, singing, a dab hand at crochet and fucking fabulous on the dance floor.

Percy's booze carburettor was going to make him a handsome fortune. But before all that, it was going to make him exceedingly drunk.

Elsie feared the wedding night might be a little underwhelming when she noticed the size of Archibald's feet.

Handkerchief at the ready,
Mr Bolfrey skipped straight
to the raciest passages.

'Yes, Daphne, I know Puggles has a cute face, but if he shits in my boudoir one more time, I swear I'll throw him in the Thames myself.'

Since the dodo incident, Gerald had sworn off psychedelics for life. Well... three months.